Marriage
LESSONS
Volume 2

Protecting and Restoring Your Marriage

Wole & Dami
Olarinmoye

Volume 2

Protecting and Restoring Your Marriage

Wole & Dami
Olarinmoye

WORD2PRINT
A Division of One-Touch Pro Ltd

MARRIAGE LESSONS: Volume 2

Copyright © 2017 Wole & Dami Olarinmoye

First published in the United Kingdom in 2017 by
Word2Print
www.word2print.com
ISBN: 978-1-908588-31-9

A CIP catalogue record for this title is available from the British Library

Edit: Karis Kolawole & Muyiwa Olumoroti

Cover design: Adeola Disu
The Kingdom Publications

Book design: Supreme Core Media
www.supremecoremedia.com

Printed and bound by
CPI Group (UK) Ltd,
Croydon, CR0 4YY

Contents

Dedication

We dedicate this book to the coming generation. May the principles we have shared here help you to choose wisely and enable you to have healthy marriages. May these principles help you to work on your marriages and reduce the divorce rate that has plagued our generation. May all our marriages be better and sweeter.

Introduction

Wise is the one who learns from another's mistakes. Less wise is the one who learns only from his own mistakes. The fool keeps making the same mistakes again and again and never learns from them. Sri Sri Ravi Shankar

Only a fool learns from his own mistakes, the wise man learns from the mistakes of others. Otto Von Bismarck

Our first book was a series of lessons we learnt in the first 18 years of our marriage. We found that our experience was proving very useful for others, hence the book was aptly titled Marriage Lessons.

Following the book, many questions arose from our readers and listeners about issues to do with common challenges plaguing many marriages. Some wondered why we had not dealt with them in our book. Our response was that we wanted to chronicle our own personal lessons, especially as there are already so many good books on marriage. The idea was not to reinvent the wheel. However, from various meetings and counselling sessions, we have come to realise that practical advice on dealing with common issues in marriage is much needed. Even if we do not have personal experience of everything, in the words of the great men above, we are to be considered wise to have learnt from the mistakes of others.

So, we bring you *Marriage Lessons* Volume 2: Protecting and Restoring Your Marriage. The first and second chapters deal with having a healthy marriage and general principles to help protect and restore your marriage using our tried and tested Marriage Health Questionnaire. The subsequent chapters are scenarios which focus on specific issues commonly responsible for causing marital discord. We show how these issues can be effectively prevented and resolved using the principles shared in chapters one and two. Although targeted primarily at married couples, singles will also greatly benefit from the principles shared here.

Enjoy!

Wole and Dami Olarinmoye
London, United Kingdom

Acknowledgments

We thank the Almighty God for the wisdom, desire, time and ability to write this second volume. Lord, without You we are nothing. Thank You.

Big thanks to Dr Muyiwa Olumoroti, our publisher, who keeps hounding us to write books and leave our mark in the sands of time. Thanks so much, bruv!

Thanks also must go to the editor, Karis Kolawole whose invaluable contribution has made this book the success story that it is. The Lord bless you real good.

We would also like to thank the very many people whose stories, suggestions, questions and enquiries following our first book on marriage have helped shape this second volume. We are eternally grateful for your role in helping us fulfil our purpose. Blessings!

1
THE HEALTHY MARRIAGE

Therefore, shall a man leave his father and his mother, and shall cleave unto his wife and they shall be one flesh. And they were both naked, the man and his wife, and were not ashamed.

The Bible

W e ended volume one of Marriage Lessons with a chapter titled, 'The Goal of Marriage'. We should probably have called it 'The Goal of a Healthy Marriage' as unfortunately people get married for many reasons, some of which do not lead to a healthy marriage. We would like to show you two dimensions of a healthy marriage. The first is a process and the second is a picture.

The process of a healthy marriage

A healthy marriage is one that is in the process of going

through or has already effectively gone through the process of leaving, cleaving and oneness.

The quote above from the Bible shows us the process a healthy marriage needs to go through. Although we discussed this in a bit more detail in Volume 1, we will briefly highlight the main points. You can get a copy of Volume 1 from Amazon and most good online book stores.

Leaving refers to dealing with the external forces that try to pull your marriage apart. This deals with everything on the outside such as family, friends, ex-relationships, work or charity commitments. These external forces are not bad in themselves but they must not be allowed to take precedence over your marriage.

Cleaving refers to dealing with the internal forces that try to prevent you from achieving oneness. This deals with everything on the inside such as differences in personality, viewpoints, background, temperament, communication and sexual appetites or preferences.

Oneness refers to the progressive move towards complete harmony and unity in your marriage, which involves being 'naked and unashamed', referring to the level of transparency required to achieve oneness.

A young marriage still in its formative phase could be healthy even though it has not completely gone through the process as it takes time. On the other hand, a couple may have been married for many years but their relationship may not be healthy if they have not effectively gone through each stage of this process.

The picture of a healthy marriage

A healthy marriage has certain qualities which certify it as healthy. The couple should be able to identify the presence and essence of these qualities even if they have only been married a short while. They are:

Commitment: The couple are totally committed to each other. They have a strong desire to make their relationship work and are prepared to put in the required effort and investment to make it happen.

Satisfaction: The couple feel satisfied with their choice of spouse and are happy with the direction their relationship is heading. There are no regrets. This does not mean there are no areas to improve upon, but there is an overall feeling of satisfaction.

Communication: The couple have learned to communicate effectively. They both feel comfortable airing their views and do not feel threatened by their spouse when they express a contrary opinion. They have regular heart to heart talks and feel comfortable in each other's company. They have understood that effective communication involves effective speaking, – speaking in a manner your spouse understands and responds to, and effective listening – listening to ensure you understand what your spouse is trying to communicate.

Conflict resolution: The couple have worked out a system of resolving conflict and differences of opinion in an amicable manner. Conflicts do not degenerate into verbal or physical violence but are properly resolved to the point of agreement.

Absence of violence and abuse: There is no physical, emotional or sexual abuse in the relationship. There is no abuse of any kind. Neither spouse feels taken advantage of in any way.

Fidelity and faithfulness: The couple do not have affairs and there is no third-party involvement. There has been no looking out, no 'extras' on the side, no wanting extras on the side. If a spouse admits they want 'extras' or have had 'extras', then an open discussion as to what is missing should be explored.

Intimacy: A healthy marriage has a good dose of both emotional and sexual intimacy. The couple enjoy being intimate first emotionally but also sexually. In emotional intimacy, you have the feeling of being loved and wanted which is extremely satisfying in itself, especially to many women. With sexual intimacy, there is the added dimension of sex and love making with the resultant effect of the sexual climax.

Friendship: The couple are best of friends. Friendship

undergirds their marriage. They are comfortable in each other's company. They like to hang out with each other and spend time together just like best friends would.

The process and picture of marriage we have painted, should always be what we aim for when we talk about a healthy marriage. If one or more of these qualities are lacking, even if there is no major problem in the marriage, you would benefit from having a time of introspection as a couple to assess why your marriage is not as healthy as it could be. Waiting for major problems is not advised. We should be proactive in protecting our marriages.

Reasons to pursue a healthy marriage

Before we round up this chapter, let us briefly remind ourselves of the reasons to pursue a healthy marriage. Some may ask, "Why bother going to such great lengths trying to have a healthy marriage? If you like the person, why not just see how it goes and if it doesn't work out, no big deal, get another one?" That may seem plausible on the surface but will unfortunately result in multiple broken relationships with the usual societal consequences of depression, single parent families, child delinquency, crime and more. Consider the following reasons to pursue a healthy marriage. They have been picked from various pieces of research on marriage and relationships.

1. Married couples in a healthy relationship live longer than their unmarried peers or those in less healthy relationships.

2. Married couples in a healthy relationship have better immune systems and are better able to fight illness and disease.

3. Married couples in a healthy relationship experience 35% less illness.

4. Married couples in a healthy relationship are less violent to themselves and to others.

5. Married couples in a healthy relationship are less likely to have mental and emotional problems.

6. Children from healthy marriages have all the benefits above (long life, better immune systems, less illness, less violence, less mental and emotional problems) and in addition:

7. Children from healthy marriages perform better academically on average.

8. Children from healthy marriages have better social skills.

9. Children from healthy marriages are more emotionally balanced.

10. Divorce is very expensive. The primary expense is emotional but it is also socially and financially expensive.

Homework:

1. Individually (not as a couple) assess your marriage using our Marriage Health Questionnaire. It is designed to fish out any area of concern in your marriage. We recommend using this questionnaire to quickly assess your marriage every 3-4 months and use it to trigger discussion. Answer 'yes', 'no' or in more detail if you like. It is your tool to use as you see fit.

Marriage Health Questionnaire

• Have I dealt with or am I progressively dealing with external forces – i.e. anything outside of both of us trying to pull us apart?

• Do I feel my spouse has dealt with or is progressively dealing with external forces?

• Have I dealt with or are am I progressively dealing with internal forces – i.e. anything that forms part of my personality, preferences or background trying to pull us apart?

- Do I feel my spouse has dealt with or is progressively dealing with internal forces?

- Am I playing my part in progressing towards oneness?

- Do I feel my spouse is playing their part in progressing towards oneness?

- Am I committed to this marriage?

- Do I feel my spouse is committed to this marriage?

- Am I satisfied in this marriage?

- Do I feel my spouse is satisfied in this marriage?

- Do I communicate well in this marriage?

- Do I feel my spouse communicates well in this marriage?

- Do I resolve conflicts well in this marriage?

- Do I feel my spouse resolves conflicts well in this marriage?

- Do I feel violated or abused in this marriage?

- Does my spouse feel violated or abused in this marriage?

- Am I faithful to this marriage?

- Do I feel my spouse is faithful to this marriage?

- Am I enjoying emotional and sexual intimacy in this marriage?

- Do I feel my spouse is enjoying emotional and sexual intimacy in this marriage?

- Do I feel we are best of friends?

- Do I feel my spouse thinks we are best of friends?

- Do I have any other concerns not mentioned above?

- Do I feel my spouse has any other concerns not mentioned above?

2. Note down any areas of concern identified. Don't do anything about them yet. The next chapter will open some general principles to help protect and restore your marriage.

3. Encourage your spouse to take the questionnaire too as an individual.

2
GENERAL PRINCIPLES TO PROTECT AND RESTORE YOUR MARRIAGE

An ounce of prevention is better than a pound of cure.
English proverb
By failing to prepare, you are preparing to fail.
Benjamin Franklin

I n this chapter, we aim to share with you, principles that will prepare you to protect your marriage even before you start. For those who have already started and have noticed some cracks here and there, this chapter will help you restore your marriage.

Preparation is extremely important prior to marriage. By failing to prepare we are unfortunately preparing to fail. In fact, we believe in an ideal world, everyone should have the opportunity to pass through a marriage preparation class to see what marriage really entails even before choosing a spouse. Many people do not really understand what marriage is about. They only think of the romance and the sex, and forget it means living with someone under the same roof for the rest of your life, taking decisions together and building a life together. Many singles decide not to progress to marriage with their previously intended spouses when they realise what marriage really means.

These are some of the questions you must ask yourself before you decide to enter into marriage:

- Do I really believe this person has my best interests at heart or is he/she only looking out for themselves?

- Will he/she help/support me to fulfil my destiny in life?

- Will he/she do his/her best to support me to be the best I can be in life?

- Am I just a source of money or really a love interest?

- Am I just a source of legitimate sex or does this person really care about me?

- Am I prepared to give myself totally and completely to this person without reservation?

- Am I making do with what is available or do I really believe that this person is my best friend and soul mate?

We believe that prevention is better than cure. If we

make the right choices and have the right mindsets from the beginning, we won't end up having to firefight bad relationships. For such an important institution as marriage, it concerns us so much that there is very little preparation available.

One of the aims of marriage preparation is to help couples look at their lives together and anticipate what potential challenges may arise because of their unique pairing, background and upbringing. A couple from different backgrounds for example, are likely to have issues arising because of cultural differences. Whose culture do they adopt as their own?

Another couple with significantly different earnings may have challenges because of decisions on how to manage money since one earns much more than the other. Who 'owns' the money since one person earns more? Does the one who earns less also have a say in how the money is spent?

Yet another couple who have had significant previous long-term relationships with or without children are likely to have issues arising because of 'imported' issues from their past. You may start to hear expressions of frustration such as: 'I feel he compares me to his/her ex-boy/girlfriend' or 'I never really wanted children, why do I have to look after his/hers?'

Awareness

The first key thing in learning to protect your marriage is awareness. The word 'awareness' is defined by the online dictionary as knowledge or perception of a situation or fact. Every couple should be aware - have the knowledge or perception of what potential issues could arise from their unique pairing. Courtship should be a time of discovery and awareness. You have already made up your mind you love this person or you feel your heart is drawn to this person; however, you also need to be aware of the potential pitfalls that could arise in future because of your unique pairing.

In our experience, many couples with challenges in marriage were aware of the issues before they became problems but either ignored them or did not deal with them properly. Every couple needs to shine the spotlight on their marriage and look for potential issues that may arise.

Openness

The second key thing in protecting your marriage is openness. Openness is defined by the online dictionary as lack of restriction, lack of secrecy or concealment, frankness. Couples need to be honest and open with each other, expose issues before they become problems and resolve them satisfactorily.

These two elements: awareness and openness are very important in protecting and restoring your marriage from the winds of life. Let us now use the example of a couple from different cultural backgrounds who choose to get married. Awareness will enable them to be observant enough to look out for differences in viewpoints or opinions about life based on their different backgrounds. Openness will prevent them from sweeping their differences under the carpet and enable them to discuss freely how those differences could potentially affect them in dealing with each other, relatives, members of the extended family and life as a whole. Another example of an issue that could arise could be: 'Should we discuss whether mum is going to live with us when she is no longer able to cope on her own or should we just sweep it under the carpet?'

Any difference of opinion, no matter how small, can either cause a rift if not resolved or contribute to resentment that will eventually boil over.

We recommend going through a sequence of five Ss to discuss your concerns. These steps can be used both to protect and restore your marriage.

Stop

Let's stop what we are doing; we have identified an issue or a potential issue. We will not sweep it under the carpet; we will not ignore it; we will not pretend it does not matter; we need to arrange a mutually convenient time and place to discuss this further.

Shine

Let's shine the light on this matter. Things hide under the cover of darkness. Light reveals things; so shine the light and let us identify exactly what the problem is. What challenges or potential challenges could our relationship have because of what we have identified? This is the time to be open and expose whatever challenges currently face our marriage or have the potential to cause problems in future.

Sit

We need to sit down together and discuss things objectively. This is not about me or you, this is about us. We have not won if I win. We have not won if you win. We only win when our marriage wins, when we both win. Although we may have different opinions, we need to find a healthy way to express them to each other. This is not the time to shout and scream. The focus is not to determine necessarily who is right or wrong. We need to ask questions like: How did we get here? What did we ignore? What did we sweep away under the carpet? What are the implications or ramifications of this situation? Although we have this situation to deal with, we need to sit down and work out what is best for us. The aim is not to hurt each other but to fully discuss the possible areas of concern.

Smooth

Having discussed fully and openly, we need to smooth things over. This is extremely important to ensure we continue to acknowledge the fact that we are on the same side. We have revealed our shortcomings. Our oversights have come to the fore. Let us now rebuild broken bridges by apologising and reaffirming our love for each other. Whatever was said in the previous stage needed to be said. Whatever was dug up in the previous stage, needed to be dug up but that does not change the fact that we love each other and are in this together for the long haul. 'Honey, I now realise that I have been taking you for granted. I did not mean it. I am so sorry and I want you to know that I really love and appreciate you. Darling, I had no idea hanging out with Bob would make you feel that way. I apologise for upsetting you and I want you to know you are number one in my life'.

Start

This is where we implement what we are going to do about what we have discovered and start the prevention or recovery process. We put together and initiate a plan of action which will ultimately set our relationship or marriage back on the path of health. In this stage, we come to a place of agreement. The recovery plan should be tested against the ideals of the Marriage Health Questionnaire where applicable. If it does not measure up, we go back to the drawing board until we arrive at something that works for both of us.

Some may ask

We have been married for quite a while and we have gotten used to and accepted 'our problem'. Isn't it too late to start assessing things now? A lot of water has gone under the bridge, should we not just let things be?

It is never too late to do the right thing and put these principles into practice. It is never too late to have a great marriage. If you have taken the Marriage Health Questionnaire and you feel something is lacking, then one sure way to start the process to restore the health of your marriage is to use the five Ss we discussed above.

In the following chapters, we will look at several scenarios certain couples found themselves in. We will use both the Marriage Health Questionnaire and the five Ss explained above to determine what could have been done to protect and what should be done to restore their marriages.

Homework:

1. Ask your spouse if they noted any concerns in the process of taking the Marriage Health Questionnaire.

2. If either of you have concerns, then arrange a mutually convenient time and place that will allow you both to be open with each other.

3. It is now time to take the concerns you have both noted from taking the Marriage Health Questionnaire and discuss those concerns in turn with each other using the five Ss. Every step is very important especially 'smooth'. You must reaffirm your love for each other and apologise where necessary. This is not a witch hunt; you are aiming for a healthier marriage.

4. If you are unable to satisfactorily resolve the concerns raised despite several discussions and re-runs of the five Ss, consider involving a marriage counsellor that you are both comfortable with, to support you through the process.

Abuse is better prevented that cured.

In 1993, The United Nations Declaration on the Elimination of Violence Against Women defined domestic violence as: Physical, sexual and psychological violence occurring in the family, including battering, sexual abuse of female children in the household, dowry-related violence, marital rape, female genital mutilation and other traditional practices harmful to women, non-spousal violence and violence related to exploitation. Although the definition leans heavily towards women being abused as these account for the vast majority of abuse cases, we know that in a few relationships, it is the men that suffer abuse. Now let us look at the scenario on the next page:

Alanita and Adonis have been married for the past seven years. While courting, Alanita observed that Adonis had a very condescending attitude. She also noticed his very bad temper, often going into a rage when he cannot have his way but she was hoping he would eventually change. Soon after marriage, he took to constantly berating her for not dressing the way he felt she should. This made her lose confidence and it affected her self-esteem. As a result, she could not bring herself to apply for various promotions at work as she felt she was not good enough. This only worsened the insults as she was now not earning as much as Adonis felt she should. Alanita is afraid to stand up to Adonis as the last time she did, he slapped her and threatened to leave her if she told anyone especially her family. Alanita is now depressed and suffers from poor motivation, low self-esteem and reduced libido. Adonis forces her to comply with his sexual demands with no consideration for her feelings, many times hurting her physically in the process. She cannot bring herself to talk to friends or family as she is ashamed and also afraid of Adonis hurting her again, especially as many had concerns about Adonis prior to their marriage. The only person who seems interested in listening to her and supporting her is Aston, an old boyfriend and work colleague...

What are the key things that stand out in this scenario?

1. Alanita is being emotionally, psychologically, physically and sexually abused. This has led to her being depressed which makes her likely to be abused even more.

2. Adonis has a very condescending attitude which Alanita noticed but did not address prior to marriage. We usually recommend that all concerns are fully addressed before marriage. If someone has a character trait you feel you cannot live with, reconsider your marriage before it is too late! Most people DO NOT CHANGE. Alanita hoped Adonis would.

3. Adonis was constantly berating Alanita for her dressing which indicates poor communication.

4. Alanita tried to stand up to him but he slapped her. At this point alarm bells should have been ringing very loudly. Violence of any kind is a big 'no go' area in marriage. Alanita should have sought external help at this point. Violence hardly ever happens just once.

5. Adonis threatened Alanita to prevent her speaking to her friends and family; which is classic abuse.

This is called divide and rule. The abuser cuts off the abused from close connections to keep them in the abused state.

6. Adonis was forcing Alanita to comply with his sexual demands with no consideration for her feelings. The likelihood is Alanita is not getting any pleasure from intimacy, which will make her feel used, abused and even more depressed.

7. Alanita has now taken to confiding in Aston, an old boyfriend and work colleague. This is not the answer unless he is pointing her in the right direction. At this time, she is vulnerable, and an easy target for a predator due to her low self-esteem. She should be speaking to someone who can give her advice about domestic abuse and depression. A good friend would have pointed her in that direction.

What could have been done to protect this marriage from abuse?

Abuse is better prevented that cured. In many cases, a person with abusive tendencies shows their true colour before marriage. We recommend that couples should deal with all the concerns they notice and resolve them before saying 'I do'. Nevertheless, if this couple had the opportunity of applying the Marriage Health

Questionnaire at an early stage - even in courtship, it would have been obvious that many very important aspects were not moving in the right direction and thus make the need for further discussion obvious. The following would have been picked up:

- Internal forces - attitude and anger of Adonis

- Progression towards oneness - not happening

- Satisfaction - absent

- Communication - poor

- Conflict resolution - very poor

- Absence of violence and abuse - not absent unfortunately

- Intimacy - very poor

This couple need to seriously reassess their marriage especially Alanita. She is being abused in several ways and unless this is urgently resolved, the right recommendation would be for her to be removed to a place of safety. That is not to say the marriage is over but a lot of work would need to be done to get this very unbalanced and very unhealthy relationship back on track. Unfortunately, many people endure abusive marriages until something goes horribly wrong.

What can be done to restore this marriage?

This will be very difficult but not impossible. It is often said that abusers have themselves been abused and either see it as normal behaviour or are themselves trapped in a cycle they are struggling to get out of. There are usually other background issues and all of that will need to be dealt with.

Let us apply the five Ss to see what should be done.

Stop

The couple need to stop! The alarm bells should have been ringing very loud and clear by now. Too many things are out of place and need to be discussed and dealt with. This marriage cannot continue in its current state. We need to apply the brakes and move to the next step.

Shine

What is the exact problem here? Why is Adonis rude and condescending? Does he view that as normal behaviour? Is that how he was treated growing up? Does he realise how Alanita feels when he speaks to her rudely? Is the issue a cultural one? Some men feel the need to impose themselves on their wives and children by being condescending. Is the issue a personality one? We also need to remember that it takes two to tango.

Has Alanita been persistently upsetting Adonis? Does she also have a role to play in this? That does not excuse the abuse but we need to shine the light on both parties to achieve proper resolution.

Sit

Now that we have shone the light and dug up the real issues, we need to sit down to discuss the problems and plan the pathway forward. Adonis may need to seek some form of counselling to help him admit, understand and deal with his aggressive nature. He will need to start treating Alanita with respect. Involving a marriage counsellor will be necessary to help navigate them through this process but they need to agree on this. This will not be an easy process. By the time violence has set into a relationship, they will likely need external help and support. Beyond the physical violence, there is also sexual violence. This is completely unacceptable. Let's put it in plain language: Adonis has been raping Alanita. He has been doing it on a regular basis, hurting her physically at times. In the Western world, he could go to jail if he is reported by Alanita.

Smooth

This is where lots of apologies and forgiveness need to take place. Alanita will certainly feel very aggrieved at how she has been used and abused; and Adonis will need to apologise for his behaviour. Alanita may also need to do the same for her part in this - whatever that is, though the burden of error appears to lie mainly with Adonis. Forgiveness will be essential especially for Alanita. Forgiveness will help to free her from resentment and bitterness which are chains to the past. The couple need to affirm and reaffirm their love and commitment to each other. This is essential to start the process of moving forward.

Start

The couple need to start afresh, implementing the plans and changes that have arisen from the discussion. This couple will likely need proper marriage counselling. Adonis may also need personal counselling to help him deal with his own personal issues that have led to being such an aggressive personality (upbringing, undetected depression, history of abuse)

IMPORTANT NOTE!!

Most abusers will not change that easily and for the security of the abused, removal to a place of safety may be required. The intervention of a marriage counsellor you can trust will be necessary in many cases. To further safeguard yourselves, we also recommend that before marriage, it is extremely important that you have someone you both respect and are accountable to. There may be times you will need this respected person to get through to you or your spouse when you are both blurred by your respective opinions. If there is no such trusted or respected person that can be called upon at that stage the relationship could be in trouble.

Marriage Lessons

- Many forms of abuse are common but completely unacceptable in any relationship especially marriage. The signs are usually there before the knot is tied, so please address them before you say, 'I do'.

- If there is a risk to the safety of the abused, they should be removed from the environment by friends or family members.

- If you are being abused, do not be afraid to ask for help from the right sources. There are many good organisations that can provide you with support and advice. Use the internet to identify and locate your local support.

- Seeking personal and marriage counselling are not signs of weakness but are evidence that you are being proactive about getting help.

- Have someone in your life that you respect, who can give you good wholesome advice in a time of crisis. Don't be a dangerous individual!

- Identify someone in the life of your spouse who they respect and can be called upon in times of crisis.

Regular time alone with a member of the opposite sex who you are not married to, nor intending to get married to is not recommended.

A dultery is defined by the online dictionary as voluntary sexual activity between a married person and someone who is not their spouse. Adultery sounds quite ugly. We could have called the chapter 'affair' or 'romantic tryst' but let's call a spade, a spade. We have used the scenario below to discuss the issue of adultery in this chapter.

Aston and Angelia have been married for two years. Since having a Caesarean section about 12 months ago, they have not had sex together. Angelia felt Aston was being 'very understanding' as he had not pressured her into having sex since she gave birth to their daughter, Amethy. She has not 'felt ready to resume sex yet'. She feels she is still recovering from the ordeal of childbirth, besides looking after their daughter. Angelia has now heard from her friend Besita, that Aston has been seen out several times with another woman, Alanita who happens to be his work colleague and old girlfriend. After confronting him repeatedly, Aston eventually admits his relationship with Alanita has become sexual in the past few months. It started off with them confiding in each other about their respective problems with their spouses and things progressed from there...

In summary, Aston has had an adulterous affair with Alanita his old girlfriend and work colleague and now Angelia feels hurt and betrayed.

What are the key things that stand out in the scenario?

1. Aston and Angelia have not had sex for 12 months. Alarm bells should have started ringing once this couple went a few months without sex. Some marriage counsellors will say weeks. That is a sign that something is wrong somewhere in the marriage and needs to be explored. Granted, she had a Caesarean section but that should have healed by six weeks unless there was an infection in which case there would have been further medical intervention.

Nevertheless, twelve months is way too long.

2. Angelia 'felt' Aston had been understanding. There had been no definite communication. She had assumed he was okay with them not having sex for 12 months! Aston himself had not brought up the issue which has resulted in harming their union.

3. Aston had been out several times with Alanita. Alarm bells should also be ringing here. What are you doing out with a woman who is not your wife, especially when it has occurred several times?

4. These outings were with an ex-girlfriend and current work colleague. Definite recipe for disaster. Calamity was screaming at Aston but he was not listening. His predatory instincts had kicked in and he was going for the goal which was emotional intimacy and eventually sex with Alanita. He was feeling 'deprived' of intimacy and sex and had found an outlet for his emotional and sexual needs.

5. Alanita and Aston had started their relationship by confiding in each other about their respective problems with their spouses. Alanita (from chapter 3) and Aston were right to communicate about their problems but were unfortunately doing so with the wrong person. Aston should have been speaking

to his spouse and Alanita should have been getting appropriate professional help.

What could have been done to protect this marriage from adultery?

Adultery is better prevented than cured. Infidelity has always been one of the top causes of marital or relationship breakdown. Studies have shown that 25-27% of divorces are caused by adultery. Although the spouse who actually commits the adultery is primarily responsible, both spouses need to assess themselves to see what part each may have played. The winds of life will blow; that is a fact. Challenges will come our way but dealing with them sooner rather than later will prevent heartache. If this couple had the opportunity to apply the Marriage Health Questionnaire at an early stage, they would have quickly noticed some major glaring concerns. We will highlight the obvious ones:

- External forces - Alanita, Amethy

- Oneness - they were growing apart

- Commitment - Aston was pursuing another relationship

- Satisfaction - Aston was not satisfied with his marriage

- Fidelity and faithfulness - Obviously lacking

- Intimacy - No sexual intimacy, probably emotional intimacy also lacking

This would have triggered a discussion and initiated communication that would likely have helped to protect this marriage from adultery. The couple would have opened up their various concerns and hopefully achieve resolution.

What can now be done to restore this marriage?

Adultery has now taken place. That in itself does not mean the end of the marriage. Yes, we do know and are very aware that it is a big thing. Stephen Covey, the author of *7 Habits of Highly Effective People* was once asked how to forgive someone who had committed adultery. He said it made him think of the prayer, 'Lord help me forgive those who sin differently than I do'. We fully accept that trust has been breached and that Aston has stepped out of line but this was a situation created by the couple and they need to deal with this situation as a couple.

Let us apply our five Ss to see what Aston and Angelia should do.

Stop

Alarm bells should have started ringing once this marriage relationship had gone more than a few months without sex. Neither of them sounded the alarm; both carried on as normal. The couple should both have been aware of the fact that while sex is very important for men, it is actually also very beneficial for women too and hugely important in the marriage relationship. It helps with unity and oneness, deepens love and affection, has multiple health benefits and more. They should both have been open enough to engage each other and discuss things. Alarm bells should also have been ringing for Aston when he started spending more and more time with Alanita. Now that adultery has taken place the bells are ringing even louder indicating that there is a problem.

Shine

We now need to ask the tough questions. What is the real problem here? Why did Angelia not feel ready to resume sex yet? Was she suffering from postnatal depression but could not express it? Was she lacking in libido? Was she upset with Aston over possible lack of support during pregnancy and childbirth? Was she afraid of getting pregnant again? Was she feeling unattractive following childbirth? Why did Aston not raise the issue and discuss it with Angelia? When Aston realised he was spending more time with Alanita, how did he justify it to himself? We should always be careful with ex-relationships, especially if they were sexual. We should even be more careful when the marriage is under strain. In fact, based on what we have seen over the years, we are bold to say that regular time alone with a member of the opposite sex who you are not married to, nor intending to get married to is not recommended as it causes undue emotional attachment. You may find yourself using the person as a source of emotional and eventually sexual intimacy. Aston was subconsciously looking for love, attention, emotional warmth and sex - as was Alanita, and they found it in each other, and both ended up in adultery.

Sit

Aston and Angelia now need to sit down and discuss the issue openly, remembering the general principles we shared in Chapter Two. Although most people would place the blame on Aston, it does take two to tango; so Angelia would need to accept some responsibility for her part in this. A frank discussion will reveal the exact nature of the problem. Maybe Angelia needed counselling, contraception or just reassurance of how much she is loved and appreciated irrespective of how she looks. Maybe Aston needed more understanding that he was not being neglected. Maybe all they needed to do was sit down and talk; it is obvious that communication was seriously lacking. We've all been there where you assume what your spouse is thinking and they had no such thing in mind. Consider the following:

'He hasn't even asked me for sex; he must think I now look ugly'.

'She hasn't initiated sex which she used to do. I really love and want her but she only cares about the baby'.

From these examples, we can see that assuming what your spouse is thinking can very easily be wrong. It is better to be open and communicate. They also need to talk about Alanita; that relationship cannot continue. Since they work together, Aston needs to find a way to reduce his contact with Alanita.

Smooth

Having talked about the problem, there will be a need for forgiveness. Aston and Angelia both feel hurt and neglected for different reasons. Love and affection needs to be reaffirmed and forgiveness needs to take place. This is extremely important. Without forgiveness, resentment will continue to build up, leading to future problems. Some may feel that what Aston has done is unforgivable but remember it was both of them that created the situation that led to this. Aston did not intentionally go out of his way to mess around. So in a sense, he is also a victim of circumstance. Yes, Aston did the wrong thing but the circumstances created by the couple in their marriage contributed heavily to it. Demonising Aston is not the answer. His actions only highlighted already existing problems which should have been detected sooner. If the couple really love each other and are willing to work at it, we recommend they proceed to the next step.

Start

They need to start again from where they are now, working through the process of a healthy marriage towards the picture of a healthy marriage. Aston needs to completely leave Alanita and cleave to his wife. They both need to be more open about each other's needs and Angelia needs to be more open about how she feels. Trust will need to be rebuilt and they may need the support of a counsellor. Aston needs to prove his loyalty and commitment by being extremely open to avoid suspicion. He should do practical things like make his mobile phone accessible to his wife and let her know of his whereabouts at all times. Security is one of the top needs of a woman; she needs to feel safe and secure especially as there has already been a breach in trust. Both attending a sexual health clinic to check for sexually transmitted diseases (STDs) may also be a practical step to take as a third party has been involved.

IMPORTANT NOTE!!

These steps will only work if both Aston and Angelia

are willing to work at it. If one of them does not feel they are prepared to go through the process, things will quickly break down. If for example, Aston chooses to blatantly or even secretly continue to engage in his extramarital affair or even other affairs, then that is a fundamental issue that will continue to compromise the marriage, making restoration very challenging.

Marriage Lessons

- Be aware of the importance of sex in a relationship.

- Many months without sex should definitely ring alarm bells unless there is a reasonable excuse or a specific health concern. Some marriage counsellors will say weeks. On average, according to research, couples in healthy marriages have sex two to three times weekly.

- Open communication is very important in a relationship.

- Regularly, frankly and openly go through the Marriage Health Questionnaire to ensure nothing is left to chance.

- Avoid very close friendships or relationships with members of the opposite sex who you are not married to, especially if your spouse is not getting that level of attention.

- Close relationships with the opposite sex or rekindling ex-relationships are best avoided. They can take away from your marriage emotionally. If you find yourself being too defensive when challenged about your relationship with a member of the opposite sex who is not your spouse, especially an old flame, alarm bells should start ringing.

Being busy can potentially put a strain on your marriage if not properly managed.

Busyness is defined by the online dictionary as the quality or condition of being busy. Many marriages will identify with the scenario below. There never seems to be enough hours in the day to do all we want to.

Bill and Besita have been married for ten years. Bill runs his own business meaning he spends long hours at work and often needs to travel away from home. He is very committed in his local church and attends every service as a member of the ushering team. Besita works full time and sings in the church choir. She also looks after their three children who are all under five. Besita has started getting increasingly stressed and is struggling to cope with the pressure she is under. This has led to frequent arguments and her marriage to Bill is becoming more and more strained...

What are the key things that stand out here?

1. Bill is very busy. You could probably call him 'Busy Bill'. He spends long hours at work, he travels a lot and when he is not travelling, he is in church. There is little or no time for the family. Alarm bells should start ringing when you have time for everything else but your family. Although his passion for service is admirable, it should not be at the expense of his family.

2. Besita is also very busy. She works full time, looks after three very young children and sings in the church choir. Her commitment is also admirable but there is no way she will have enough time for the children and her husband running that type of schedule. Alarm bells should be ringing very loud.

3. Besita is getting stressed and struggling to cope. This will invariably lead to outbursts of frustration and anger along with raised voices, which will further worsen things.

4. Frequent arguments have started to occur and the marriage is becoming strained. Unfortunately, their busyness has encroached on the time they should spend together to strengthen their marriage relationship. Although the couple do not appear to have a major problem, this marriage is slowly drifting in the wrong direction. Their energy and focus are on external things and this can eventually become a problem if left unchecked.

What could have been done to protect this marriage from the negative effects of busyness?

There is nothing wrong with being busy; it is a reality of modern life. The real issue is making sure that your busyness does not negatively impact your marriage and family life.

The Marriage Health Questionnaire will reveal that the following areas may be lacking:

- Leaving - lots of external forces arising from commitment to children, church and work

- Cleaving - internal forces of frustration

- Satisfaction - lacking

- Communication - poor

- Conflict resolution - poor

- Intimacy - likely to be suffering if always arguing and too busy

- Friendship - lacking

The discovery of these issues should trigger a discussion to help the couple manage their schedule in order to ensure their family life is protected. Solutions such as reducing work commitments by one or both spouses may help. Reducing commitment to additional extra-curricular activities may also be required. The important thing is to have a discussion and arrive at a solution that would benefit the marriage.

What can be done to restore this marriage?

This couple have started to have arguments, things are strained and beginning to break down. Let us apply our five Ss to see what they should do.

Stop
Although this may appear to be the life many people are used to, there are obvious signs of strain that are better dealt with now to prevent a bigger problem later. You

may think your job role or church responsibility is so important that everything will crumble if you are not there; think again. No one is indispensable, take time out to deal with things before it is too late. The key is still awareness. We found ourselves in a very similar position and we had to use this same process to resolve things. You can read more about this in our first book on marriage called *Marriage Lessons Volume 1*. Don't continue like this; prevention is better than cure. Do not wait for things to degenerate completely before you do something about it. The frequent arguments are an indication that Bill and Besita need to apply the brakes and stop!

Shine

What is the real problem here? Is Bill getting proper value from his very busy business? Does he appreciate the importance of spending time at home rather than spending family time elsewhere? Is Bill consciously or unconsciously running away from home? Does he find dealing with work easier than dealing with young children? Besita is getting stressed with all she has to cope with. It is not easy to look after three young children, work full time, commit to a church choir and be a wife all at the same time. Is Besita being an effective mother? Is she an effective employee? Are the children being neglected? Something will start to give sooner or later. She obviously does not get much help from Bill who is very busy with work and church. The couple may not appear to be doing anything wrong but life is happening to them and they are not prioritising their marriage and family. Not doing anything about their challenges is not an option.

Sit

The couple need to sit down and discuss their options. Their marriage and family life is suffering, and if this goes on, it will impact on the children and their lives as a whole. Work could eventually start to suffer; mistakes can be made which could be costly especially if they do safety critical work. When we faced a similar situation we sat down, discussed various options, and we eventually concluded that Dami working full time was not compatible with our busy lifestyle. We considered other practical options like using a laundry service, house cleaners, gardeners to relieve the pressure on us. We were blessed and fortunate to be in a position whereby we could afford to 'buy in' help. However, we are aware that a lot of people may not be in that position. You have to decide on what is best for you. We also worked on reducing our church commitments in order to prioritise our marriage. At a point, Wole was a leader in two very busy teams in church as well as being a home group leader with extra involvement in some other teams. Dami was also in two teams. Following an open discussion, we trimmed down our external commitments and prioritised our marriage. Bill and Besita need to have a similar discussion and work out what is best for them as a couple and family.

Smooth

The couple need to smooth things over. They need to reaffirm their love for each other and apologise for taking each other for granted. In our case, Wole felt Dami was unappreciative of all the hard work he was doing to ensure the family was comfortable. Dami on the other hand felt Wole was unsupportive and taking Dami for granted for all the work she was doing to keep the home running properly. In smoothing things over, we reconciled and learned to be more appreciative and supportive of each other. This on its own worked wonders. Even before we implemented the changes, we felt a revitalisation in our marriage because we both felt supported and appreciated.

Start

Bill and Besita need to implement their 'game plan' and put into operation whatever they have concluded is the way forward for their marriage and lives. For us, it was Dami going part-time in addition to the support and appreciation we gave each other. We realised that when we worked out the cost of getting people to do various things for us - child care, gardening, laundry, house cleaners, it was more cost effective doing it ourselves.

That may not be a feasible option for all. It is important that you both agree on works best for your marriage and then implement the process.

Marriage Lessons

- There is nothing wrong with being busy but it can potentially put a strain on your marriage if not properly managed. Being aware of it will enable you to take more care to prevent problems before they set in.

- Do not take each other for granted. Being regularly physically and verbally supportive and appreciative goes a long way to improve your cohesion. Consider romantic gestures like sending regular text messages showing love and appreciation.

- Extra commitments, church, club or other charity involvements need to be balanced against the needs of your marriage and support in the home. Family life should take priority and precedence before other external commitments.

- Joining up with friends and family can also be helpful if they live nearby. If you have friends with children of similar ages, you can support each other and baby sit for each other.

6
CHILDREN

The important thing in having and raising children is agreeing together and working together.

———————————————

Children are a blessing from the Lord. However, it is important that we are aware that children - or the lack thereof can potentially put your life and marriage under a lot of strain. A very well-known politician in the UK divorced his wife over issues to do with how to bring up their children. Please do not take this for granted.

Bill and Besita whom we looked at in the last chapter initially struggled to have children. They had three years of anxiety before eventually having three children in just over four years. The initial stress of not conceiving has now been replaced by the stress of having to cope with three young children. Both Bill and Besita are now frightened of having more children so they avoid sex. They also have very different views about how to bring up children. This often results in frequent arguments which is also putting their marriage under strain...

What are the key things that stand out from this scenario?

1. Any prolonged period of difficulty having children can take its toll on a relationship. The strain of unfulfilled expectations, disappointments, hospital visits for tests can be overwhelming. There can also be resentment if one spouse is the obvious cause (for example, a man with low sperm count or a woman with an inadequate menstrual cycle).

2. Three children in four years! They were very busy! Children are a blessing but this means Besita has basically spent a three to four-year period continuously having and nursing children. This is very stressful and will put a strain on the marriage. As beautiful as children are, pregnancy can be a very difficult period which requires great understanding. With the quick succession of pregnancies and children, this is bound to put some strain on the marriage.

3. Having had children in rapid succession, they are now afraid of having more children, and avoid sex rather than speak to their doctor about contraception.

4. The couple have different views about bringing up children. One person might say "We went through so much to have these children; please let them have whatever they want". The other will reply, "That's the more reason we should discipline them well so they turn out right".

5. The cumulative unresolved stresses over the years is taking its toll and the marriage is now under strain.

What could have been done to protect this marriage?

We recommend that couples discuss and agree on as many things as possible to do with children. How many children do you want to have? What happens if you have only boys or only girls? Will you continue trying until you have a different gender? Is that really necessary? We need to bear in mind that one cannot prepare for challenges such as delayed conception, challenging pregnancies, difficult children, disabled children or multiple births, either together or in a short space of time. All these will cause some degree of strain. Add to that your different views on raising children and this can be a big source of stress.

Left to Wole, our girls would play with him most of the time, watch movies and rush homework and housework. Left to Dami, all homework and housework must be done first and then squeeze in play time only if available. Our different views are partly due to who we are. Wole is the last child in his family and Dami is the first girl in her family. Wole can be quite laid back and Dami is very passionate about housework and school work. After having several disputes about this, we agreed that both our views had their valid points. We have now implemented a hybrid of both. Children definitely need discipline and structure but they also need time to play and enjoy their childhood.

Early application of The Marriage Health Questionnaire would have shown Bill and Besita that they need to work on the following areas:

- External forces - the children

- Internal forces - their different viewpoints

- Communication

- Conflict resolution

This would have resulted in discussions aimed at resolving their concerns about having and raising children.

What can be done to restore this marriage?

Though things are not that bad at the moment, they can definitely improve and so only slight adjustments should be required. Let us apply the five Ss.

Stop

The frequent arguments should have started ringing alarm bells. We should all be aware of the impact children can have on a marriage or even the impact of not having children. Children are an important part of the family but the absence or presence of children should not be a cause for marital breakdown. In many cultural settings, if a woman does not conceive, her husband goes off to 'pastures new'. Bill and Besita should have noticed that many of their arguments originate from the issues they have with children. They need to apply the brakes and start the process.

Shine

What is the real cause of strain? In the case of delayed conception, does one person feel aggrieved by the other for some reason? Is there any resentment over previous promiscuous behaviour or medical intervention that may have led to this? Is it the different views of bringing up children? Is one party insisting their way of raising the children is better? Is it just the sheer strain of having to cope with many young children at the same time? Bill and Besita have probably not sat down to have a productive discussion about how they can work together to bring up their children. This would be the next logical step.

Sit

Again, the key here is openness and working together. Right from the beginning (in an ideal world), there should be adequate planning for children, with medical advice sought for family planning to avoid the strain and stress of unplanned pregnancies. In the case of protracted difficulties in conceiving, both need to openly consider alternatives such as adoption and the various forms of assisted conception available (IVF). Unfortunately, these alternatives are openly or secretly frowned upon by many of African origin. (Not so much in other cultures.) Some people deem not having children as a failure and adopting or having assisted conception as accepting that failure. Others prefer to agree on applying religious/spiritual approaches (faith and prayer, for example) without any recourse to the use of medicine. The important thing is agreeing together and working together. Bill and Besita need to sit down, freely and openly discuss their differences and agree on what they plan to do going forward.

Smooth

The arguments would have taken their toll, so never forget this important step in the process, smoothing things over. Reaffirm love for each other and apologise where necessary for negative views, comments and even resentments. Bill and Besita need to resume having sex with adequate contraception, or that will open the doors to yet more problems in their marriage.

Start

The 'game plan' should now be implemented as previously discussed. Practical steps to harmonising their views on bringing up children such as reading books, creating time, getting appropriate help etc should be put in place.

Marriage Lessons

- Children are a blessing but if not properly managed, the desire for children and the rearing of children can place considerable strain on the marriage.

- Pregnancy itself can be stressful. The woman goes through many different feelings, cravings, aching and much more. This can be a stressful period, especially if the pregnancy is a difficult one. The husband needs to show a lot of understanding at this time.

- Children should be planned for to ensure they are born into a loving and welcoming environment. This will also reduce the strain on the marriage relationship.

- The couple should discuss and agree on how to bring up their children to avoid unnecessary arguments. This should be done as soon as possible in the marriage or even prior.

- For those having challenges conceiving, adoption and assisted conception are valid alternatives, which can also bring happiness to the family. There is absolutely nothing wrong with choosing to 'go spiritual' and applying faith and prayer but you can make a child happy by being available to foster or adopt. Dami knows a lady who adopted an abandoned child many years ago. She had been trying to conceive and was going through various treatments which were thought to have been unsuccessful. She was very wealthy and she decided to look after this child like her own. Within a short space of time, she fell pregnant and had her own baby. Her doctors believed that the stress of trying to conceive had taken its toll on her but when she focused on another child, her body relaxed and she took in.

7
CROSS-CULTURAL RELATIONSHIPS

Alarm bells should ring where there are cultural or religious differences even if they are subtle.

Cross-cultural is defined by the online dictionary as relating to different cultures, and is a much more common situation than many people realise. Although the scenario used below relates to Zambia and England, cross-cultural challenges can also apply to people from the same country but from different tribes or regions. For example, there are subtle cultural differences between the Scottish and the English but very significant cultural differences between many African tribes that belong to the same country. Religious differences can also be lumped under this section even those within the same faith. In Christianity for example, one may be orthodox while the other spouse could be Pentecostal or Catholic and this could create its own tensions if differences arise. In Islam, you have the Sunni and Shia Muslims. These cultural or religious differences can cause tensions in the nuclear and extended family. Therefore it is important to have a candid discussion early in the relationship about beliefs, values and ways of doing things influenced by your culture. Now consider this scenario as an example.

Ched and Cally have been married for two years. Ched is from Zambia while Cally is English. They met at university and after dating for a few years they got married. Cally feels somewhat uncomfortable and left out when Ched is with his family and friends as she does not understand his language, which he speaks freely when he is with them. Cally does not feel she has been fully accepted by Ched's family, especially his mother, Conita, who often comes around to stay many times without notice. Conita always seems to have something she is not happy about regarding the state of the house, the lack of cultural food and she definitely blames Cally for the couple's decision to delay having children for a few years. Ched is quite laid back about it all but Cally is beginning to feel trapped...

What are the key things that stand out from this scenario?

1. The couple are from different cultures. This on its own will throw up a lot of potential conflict situations due to the differences in background, upbringing and preferences like food, places, friends; etc.

2. Cally feels uncomfortable and left out especially when Ched is with his friends and family. Ched and family/friends speak their native language which Cally does not understand. It is natural to feel left out if you do not understand what is being said. In fact, you may sometimes start to wonder if people are talking about you.

3. Cally does not feel fully accepted by Ched's circle of family and friends which makes her feel isolated.

4. Cally and Conita (Ched's mum) are not getting on very well. Conita probably did not want Cally to marry her son, preferring him to marry someone from the same culture. This is showing up as Conita picking holes in all Cally does to prove her 'inadequacy' to Ched.

5. Ched and Cally have chosen to delay having children; which is anathema in many African cultures, upsetting Conita even more. It is perfectly acceptable

in the Western world to delay having children or even choose not to have any at all.

6. Cally is feeling trapped, which invariably means she will either start complaining or lashing out or she will withdraw into a shell which are all negative forms of expressing concerns.

7. Conita comes around to stay often and many times without notice! We do not recommend this at all if it can be helped, especially in a young marriage.

8. What about Cally's family? They seem to have been left out of the picture which is likely contributing to her isolation.

What could have been done to protect this marriage?

The couple have not done anything wrong by getting married but they need to be aware of the unique challenges of cross-cultural relationships. Alarm bells of caution and care should be ringing just because they are from different cultures. Studies carried out in America by the PEW research centre have shown that inter-racial marriages have a significantly higher chance of ending up in divorce in almost all cases. The only exception was in marriages between African

American women and white men which was actually 44% lower. These statistics were in comparison to white and white marriages. The point here is that of awareness. If as a couple, you are aware of the potential pitfalls, you can take steps to guard against them.

Before the feeling of being trapped set in, early application of the Marriage Health Questionnaire would have revealed the following areas of concern:

- External forces - Ched's friends and family especially his mum, Conita.

- Internal forces - different backgrounds and cultural preferences.

- Communication - not talking about the issues.

- Conflict resolution - taking Cally's concerns for granted or ignoring them.

This would have triggered the relevant discussions that would have protected this marriage from strain.

What can be done to restore this marriage?

Let us apply the five Ss.

Stop

We should all be aware that cross-cultural relationships will present their unique challenges. This does not mean we should not have cross-cultural relationships, but it does mean that we should be more aware of potential challenges such as the ones highlighted. Alarm bells should ring where there are cultural or religious differences even if they are subtle. This couple need to stop and put in place some form of resolution.

Shine

The obvious problem is that the couple are from different cultures but it is a bit more than that. Ched is not being considerate of the fact that Cally feels left out of discussions. Ched is also not doing anything to protect Cally from Conita who appears to be bullying her and finding fault in everything she does. Cally is feeling 'trapped' and she does not appear to have addressed it with Ched, or she may have and he has not taken it seriously.

Sit

The couple need to sit down to discuss the issues before things get out of hand. They may want to consider taking decisions like, 'No native (in this case African) language should be spoken while Cally is around' to make her feel included in all discussions. If Ched's friends or family cannot speak English, then Ched needs to interpret for Cally to make her feel included. Cally could also consider making the effort to learn Ched's language as this would make her feel better about relating to her husband's friends and family. Ched needs to shield Cally from Conita's bullying and fault finding. He needs to make it clear that Cally is his choice and that should be respected.

A woman needs security and at the moment, Cally does not feel secure in her own home. Ched also needs to make it clear that their choice to delay having children is a joint one and Cally should not be blamed for it. Even if it was her idea in the first place, it was a joint decision. If it wasn't then that needs to be discussed. Nevertheless, they need to discuss the best way to pass the message across to avoid a backlash on Cally. We usually recommend that each spouse should be responsible for dealing with their own family as this is less likely to be misconstrued.

Smooth

Ched and Cally need to reaffirm their love and commitment to each other. Ched especially needs to let Cally to know how much he loves her. Cally feels aggrieved and needs to let go of her hurts and smooth things over with Ched to keep their marriage relationship healthy.

Start

The couple need to implement the outcome of their discussion and plans to secure and solidify their marriage. A major part of this would be having a discussion with Conita. It is important that she is not alienated or made to feel unwelcome as ultimately, in her own way, she wants what is best for Ched. However, her meddling and interference does need to be addressed and Ched is the best person to do so. If Cally tries to do it, she will be branded as rude and disrespectful. It must fall to each spouse to manage their own family members. We do not recommend family members staying over in the early part of the marriage, especially the first year, to allow proper bonding time. You need your personal time and space to develop your relationship and get to know each other better.

IMPORTANT NOTE!!

Ched and Cally need to resolve these cross-cultural issues preferably before children arrive. They need to agree on the culture their children will be brought up in; or even an understanding of both cultures. Things like what to call elders – in the UK, children call their parents friends by name which would be presumed rude by those of African origin. For children of African parentage, anyone who is significantly older is referred to as 'auntie' or 'uncle' as a mark of respect even if not directly related. None of these are right or wrong, just different cultures. For those with religious differences – and this applies even within the same religion, some agreement should be reached as to what will become the family way of worship to avoid conflict later on. The couple have the liberty to pick and choose from both cultures to get a sensible hybrid that works for their family.

Marriage Lessons

- Cross-cultural relationships will come with challenges which you should be aware of and protect your marriage against.

- Expressed concerns by the more isolated spouse must be taken seriously to avoid feelings of being trapped and alone.

- Ground rules for dealing with cross-cultural challenges should be established early on, which will be a template for managing any challenges that arise. These include discussions over language spoken, interpreting for the non-speaker's benefit, attempts to learn the language, managing family members etc.

- Family and friends should not be 'ditched' as they usually mean well, but they must still be nicely and respectfully managed.

Money will always be a potential source of conflict in marriage.

Disparity in earnings, career, professional and social progress and development can be a major cause of marital strain. We have had many ladies asking questions about how to manage situations in which they earn more or are more highly placed than their husbands. The scenario below may help illustrate some of these challenges.

Frank and Felicity have been married for five years from just after university. Felicity has also done a Masters degree and some other courses and now earns almost twice as much as Frank who has not developed himself. Frank is becoming resentful of Felicity's success and he feels she does not respect him because she earns more. Felicity feels Frank is preventing her from developing further and achieving her career goals. She has been offered a director's role in her company but Frank feels she should turn it down as her career is affecting their marriage.

What are the key things that stand out from this scenario?

1. Felicity has pursued career development and progression and is now reaping the rewards resulting in her earning much more than Frank.

2. Frank has not developed himself. We wonder why. Lack of opportunity? Laziness? Other challenges? Undiagnosed depression?

3. Frank is becoming resentful of Felicity's success which seems unfair. She has worked hard to develop herself and progress. Many men try to subdue and hold back their wives by forcing the issue of 'respect' and 'submission'. This can be a sign of inferiority complex and is common in men of African and Asian origin, some Alpha type males of Caucasian origin and those with strong religious tendencies.

4. Frank is now actively holding Felicity back from progressing in her career. This is wrong. They both stand to gain and benefit from her promotion and success. Why hold her back just to make yourself feel

better? This could also be a subtle form of emotional abuse.

5. However, is it possible that Felicity has gotten so carried away with her career development that she is neglecting her husband? One wonders why Frank is so angry. Is this different from what was discussed?

What could have been done to protect this marriage?

We recommend that couples grow and develop together. Alarm bells should start ringing when one person wants to make progress and the other doesn't. The more progressive spouse should encourage the other to keep developing. Ongoing development is good for the brain and mental health and will strengthen your relationship if done together.

Development need not be restricted to studying courses alone as not everyone has the same academic capability but it is important to find ways to improve yourself and make yourself more valuable at work or in whatever you do professionally.

Application of the Marriage Health Questionnaire would have shown a few areas of concern that would need considering to protect this marriage:

• External forces - work and money

- Internal forces - attitude to life and progress

- Satisfaction – they both seem to be satisfied with different things with respect to career development which was causing some strain.

- Communication

- Conflict resolution

What can be done to restore this marriage?

It will involve discussions about money, spending, budgeting, personal allowances, career development and aspirations. Let us apply the five Ss.

Stop

Money will always be a potential source of conflict in marriage. Alarm bells should have been ringing once the income disparity had started to show itself. This is not necessarily bad, there are many marriages where there is an earning disparity. In fact, these days, it is not uncommon for some women earn more than their husbands. We must remember that money is not the only item we contribute to marriage. A couple may be comfortable with one person earning significantly less, if they have discussed it and agreed on it, even if it is the man that earns less. Nevertheless, all money and career progress disparities should trigger a discussion about the future. In this scenario, Frank and Felicity need to apply the brakes and start the process.

Shine

What exactly is the problem here? Is Frank just lazy or does he genuinely find studying difficult? Could Frank be a very content individual who is happy with where he is and not particularly worried about joining the rat race of life? Is Felicity being too pushy about progress? What is behind the resentment? Does Frank feel Felicity is flaunting her success and new found earning potential? Maybe Frank does not like his job but is too scared to consider a career change. Does Frank feel ashamed or have low self-esteem? All this needs to be openly explored.

Sit

Once the exact nature of the problem has been identified, the couple need to discuss the details and try to work out what is best for their marriage. It is unlikely that turning down an opportunity to achieve professional or career progress and bring more money into the family will be the right choice, nevertheless the couple need to arrive at that decision for themselves. It is important that Frank does not bring personal or cultural sentiments into the discussion. Many believe that the man should earn more but should the woman then intentionally earn less? If the couple really believe they are one and are working together then does it really matter who brings in what, or how much, as long as the marriage and family are doing well? The couple will need to discuss the implications of Felicity becoming a director. Will she feel ashamed of him, when she needs to take him with her to company functions? Would he feel ashamed accompanying her? Would she commit to her work more than the marriage given a new status in the company? Would Frank be happy for her to attend late night meetings or travel long distance for work purposes? All this would need to be discussed.

Smooth

Once again it is very important to smooth things over. Reaffirming love and apologising for hurting each other's feelings is very important for the health of the marriage. Frank needs to apologise for trying to undermine Felicity's progress and for his own lack of advancement. Felicity may need to apologise for not understanding what Frank may be going through in his own job that may be affecting his growth and development or why he may be feeling threatened. They both need to affirm their love for each other as this is essential for the health of their marriage.

Start

They need to implement what they have agreed on such as maybe Frank changing jobs or starting a course and allowing Felicity to become a Director but understanding the implications - longer hours, possible travel, evening meetings etc.

IMPORTANT NOTE!!

This may be a bitter pill to swallow for some, but it is recommended that married couples ideally have a joint account and take time to discuss their spending together as a couple. In a healthy marriage, the family income is the family income irrespective of who it comes through. For those not used to this, it should be both a process and a project. It is an ideal to attain to but will require trust and communication. We believe that if a couple can work out their differences when it comes to money, then they can probably work most things out. We recommend having a joint account for general expenses and then personal accounts into which you are both paid monthly spending allowances for lunch, emergency spending and such like. It is usually accepted that ladies get a slightly higher monthly allowance (sorry guys!) for their hair, manicure, clothes, shoes and toiletries as men do not need as much (generally speaking) but there will be variations.

Marriage Lessons

- Growth and development is good but disparity in earnings and position in society can cause conflict which should be anticipated, discussed and resolved.

- We should encourage each other to grow professionally and financially.

- True oneness as a couple should include oneness in financial affairs.

9
MONEY

All the income in a household belongs to the family; it does not matter that one person earns a lot more than the other.

We would like to delve a bit deeper into the issue of money which causes a lot of disputes in marriage. The root of most financial or money problems in marriage is in our next statement:

'My money belongs to me'.

Nope, in a healthy marriage it doesn't! The language changes in a healthy marriage. Use of 'our' and 'we' takes over from 'I' and 'me'. When you are truly one as you ought to be in marriage, you will not say this is mine or that is yours, but rather all things are ours.

Forget what your mother told you: *"As a woman, you must hide some money from your husband to safeguard yourself"*. Forget what your dad told you: *"As a man, you cannot let your wife know about all the money you have; she will spend it all".*

None of these mindsets are productive or constructive in a healthy marriage. Your money does not belong to you. It is exactly this kind of thinking that creates the following problems:

- I discovered my spouse has been making investments I was not aware of.

- I discovered my spouse is buying or building property without my knowledge.

- I discovered my spouse sends all his/her money to his/her family every month and makes me pay all the bills and tells me he/she has no money.

- I don't know how much my spouse earns; payslips are always hidden.

The statements described above should set off alarm bells. This only happens when someone thinks their money belongs to them. The state of affairs represented by the statements above is deceitful. Why should your spouse not know how much you earn or what you are building/investing? Why are such things hidden between you?

All the income in our household belongs to the family. It does not matter that one person earns a lot more than the other. It is our money and we both sit down together to budget and agree on how best to spend it for the good of the family. Let us not forget that as important as money is, it is not the only important input into a relationship or family. Other inputs such as housework, looking after children, shopping and other household chores are also important.

However, we are not naive. We are aware some people cannot trust their spouses with money; some spouses cannot trust themselves with money; some have been betrayed in the past and are still paying off debts as a result. So, how can this be managed? Every situation needs to be managed individually but the rule of thumb is openness. Couples should work towards openness and oneness in financial affairs by declaring all income that comes in and they should work towards agreeing on how the money should be spent.

As a couple, we agree on all major spending. Until we agree, the project stays on hold. If one of us feels very strongly about a project or an investment, it is that person's role to highlight the benefits of the project and carry the other along. We make agreement an absolute priority in our marriage. It forces effective communication, discussion and reconciliation.

So how can we deal with financial problems in marriage? Apply the five Ss.

Stop
Apply the brakes, stop all projects, let's start the process of coming to a place of agreement.

Shine

Let there be light. What exactly is the problem? Does one spouse have problems with spending money, being too frugal, or even laziness? Is someone hiding money away? Are there secret projects? Can there be trust again? Are we maximising all our earning potential? Are we saving the right amount of money?

Sit

Let's fully discuss the issues. Why is there a lack of trust? Is there a track record of poor spending on someone's part? Are childhood experiences influencing how we deal with finances? Who should we appoint as the 'financial director'?

Smooth

Never forget to apologise and reaffirm love and commitment. Feelings may have been hurt with what has just been said so it is very important to smooth things over with love and forgiveness.

Start

It's time to put into practice what we have decided to do. This will involve practical things like:

- Rebuilding trust. What can I initially trust you with? This might mean starting from little and building up slowly.

- Appoint a 'financial director'. Let the more trusted spouse keep an eye on the income and expenditure to ensure balance. This should also include savings and investments. No matter how little, don't use up all your income, save and invest some! Have agreed rules on what you will use your savings for. Remember the more you agree on, the less room there for conflict.

- Are you part of your company pension scheme?

- If you are big earner consider income protection to safeguard your income against periods when you cannot work.

- Have an allowance. Some people will 'die' if they have no money to spend. Agree on a monthly allowance for spending.

- Involve a mediator if necessary, who understands how finance should work in marriage.

- Don't tie your happiness to money; remember that the best things in life are free: friendship, love, romance and loyalty. This is a quote from our first book on marriage, *Marriage Lessons*.

- Finally, remember the goal of marriage is oneness, work towards oneness in finance by learning to have all things in common and agreeing on all major spending. We use the phrase, 'major spending' as many men will not agree with all their wives choose to spend money on. Have an agreed amount that frees rather than shackles your wife. We accept that this is a generalisation as in some relationships, it is the man who is the spender.

10
SEX

Until your mind is renewed to see sex in the proper way, it will be difficult to engage and enjoy sex properly.

W̲e have a feeling this may be the first chapter you have turned to! That's ok, sex intrigues us all!

We would also like to delve a bit deeper into sexual problems in marriage. In our experience of working with couples, one of the major problems we encounter is some form of sexual incompatibility. This is a situation in which there is some disparity between the sexual drive or preferences of the couple. Although not a good enough excuse for infidelity, leaving the incompatibility issue unresolved, will create an opening that can lead to further problems. It is one of the issues in which cleaving must take place - resolving sexual differences. For a reminder or better understanding of what cleaving is, please see chapter one or *Marriage Lessons Volume 1*.

Certain mindsets or situations can contribute to sexual incompatibility and problems such as:

1. Sex is only (or mainly) for men.

2. I am doing you a favour giving you sex.

3. You are insatiable or undisciplined if you regularly ask for sex; why can't you control yourself more?

4. I hate sex as it reminds me of previous (or current) negative experiences e.g. rape, sexual abuse.

5. I don't like the way you do it with me; my ex was better at it than you are.

6. I don't like the way you do it with me; it looks better on TV/the internet (pornography).

7. I am not getting enough sex; my needs are not being met.

8. I hardly ever climax; what is wrong with me?

9. I am no longer as hard as I used to be; what is wrong with me?

10. We like having sex but we are so busy that we don't have time.

11. My husband is a good man; he doesn't bother me for sex (who is he bothering?)

12. Sex is not important; what matters is that we love each other. (Really?)

Where do we start? Each situation needs to be managed on its own merit but let us start with looking at some benefits of sex according to scientific research. The act of sex releases various hormones including oxytocin and endorphins with various health and psychological benefits according to research.

1. It enhances unity, oneness and agreement.

2. It enhances emotional warmth, closeness and intimacy.

3. It encourages communication.

4. It encourages conflict resolution.

5. It promotes relaxation, stress relief and good sleep.

6. It helps with pain relief.

7. The act of sex burns calories and helps with heart health and lowering blood pressure (Twice weekly sex cuts the risk of heart attacks by 50%).

8. It strengthens your immune system and helps you fight off illnesses including cancer.

9. In women, sex improves bladder function.

10. In men, sex reduces the risk of prostate cancer.

11. It improves general functioning and wellbeing.

12. It reduces depression and promotes happiness.

From the benefits stated above, you can see that sex is not for men or for women; it is for both of you and for your marriage. When done properly and in love, it enhances and creates oneness, togetherness, emotional warmth and depth. The list goes on.

Sex starts in the mind. Until your mind is renewed to see sex in the proper way, it will be difficult to engage and enjoy sex properly. The negative mindsets listed above must be dropped and replaced with positive mindsets. If any of those mindsets are a problem then you must discuss them. If you feel discussing them with your spouse will be difficult then please find a good marriage counsellor you can trust to discuss and resolve the issues.

Openness and communication are also extremely important in letting your spouse know what you want and don't want, and what you will both allow and will not allow in your sexual relationship. If you are psychologically scarred from a previous negative sexual experience such as rape or comparing your spouse to a previous sexual partner, then you may need help from a marriage counsellor. Though not easy, you cannot allow the past to dictate your present or future.

Many men, and an increasing number of women are dependent on or addicted to pornography and use it for their sexual gratification. Reasons given are previous exposure to sexual images when growing up, curiosity, insufficient sex from spouse, deviant sexual appetites, history of sexual abuse, ashamed of high sex drive. Some people feel dirty for wanting a lot of sex so they look for alternatives but this is not the solution.

Pornography is a lie. Unfortunately, many believe what is taking place in those abhorrent pornographic images and videos, and want to reproduce the athletic and acrobatic moves in their own love making, resulting in disappointment and let down. This takes away from your marriage, making your sexual experience less satisfying. What many of those who are deceived by pornographic acts don't realise is that many of the actors are hooked on unbelievable amounts of performance drugs to help them perform. They also rely on recreational drugs to help them cope with the emotional and psychological aftermath of their extreme portrayals. Avoid pornography and watch your sex life improve. If you are addicted and need help, speak to a marriage counsellor for advice. One rule of thumb is 'feed it, grow it; starve it, kill it'. The more you watch, the more you will want to watch and the worse the longing for pornography will be; but if you starve it, it will slowly but surely start to die and the longing will fade. If you cannot trust yourself, then please make yourself accountable to someone you can trust who will support you through the process.

Problems with libido, climaxing or erectile dysfunction can be discussed with an experienced counsellor, sex therapist or a general practitioner. Various reasons such as stress, medication, medical conditions, past operations can be responsible and managed accordingly. A history of previous female genital mutilation (barbaric and unnecessary circumcision for women) can also be responsible for problems climaxing. If any of these problems are a cause for concern, please do speak to your general practitioner and you will be given appropriate guidance.

Final Thoughts

We hope you have enjoyed this book but more importantly, found in it something useful to help strengthen your marriage and make it healthier. We are now in our 20th year of marriage but we have discovered over the years that we cannot outgrow the basic principles we have shared in this and our previous book on marriage (*Marriage Lessons*).

Marriage is like the Garden of Eden. Although beautiful, you need to constantly cultivate it, pay attention to it, develop it, watch over it, be aware of the lurking dangers and protect it, to ensure you keep enjoying its beauty and fruit.

Divorce is not the answer to an unhealthy marriage. Many couples have jumped into divorce with its immense emotional, social and financial implications and realised the grass is not always greener on the other side. Sometimes taking the pain to work through the five Ss repeatedly is well worth the rewards rather than you and your children suffering the emotional, social and financial strain of separation and divorce. We know some of you reading this book may have felt you had no choice but to go down the route of divorce, and we do understand that it can be a difficult place to be; but with some commitment, dedication and a lot of hard work we believe these practical principles will help others protect and restore their marriage.

We have worked with many couples on the brink of separation and divorce and we know from experience it is possible to restore troubled marriages.

We must say again that when there is significant and continuous abuse in a relationship, whether physical, emotional or sexual, it is difficult to justify a man or woman staying in it. We are not advocating divorce but we are saying the abused should immediately be removed to a place of safety. This may be contrary to many religious opinions but when you have seen people hurt, psychologically damaged or killed because of abuse, you cannot justify asking someone to stay in those circumstances.

Regularly use the Marriage Health Questionnaire to assess your marriage health and remember to talk openly, freely but not rudely about all concerns. We recommend using it every 3-4 months as part of your quarterly review.

Well, that's it! We wish you every blessing in your marriage and life as a whole. Blessings!

Wole and Dami

Here to help

We have written *Marriage Lessons Volume 2* as a service to this generation. The scenarios in this book may have raised a lot of questions for you, making you feel like we were reading your mail. If that is the case, the simple tools we have shared here will be of great help to you. If however, you do have further pressing questions about your relationship or marriage, or about anything you have read in this book, you can contact us via our website www.decasections.org or *woleolarinmoye.com* and we would be more than willing to tackle any questions you may have.

We look forward to hearing from you.

Wole and Dami Olarinmoye

www.decasections.org

Another book from Decasections.org

The Decasections of Life

Author: Wole Olarinmoye

ISBN-13: 978-1-908588-10-4

Format: Paperback, Pages: 168

Book information

Do you sometimes feel deficient in one or more areas of your life? Do you feel that there is more to life than you are currently experiencing? Have you ever wondered if there were certain boxes in your life you are not yet ticking? Are you aware that there are at least ten areas of your life which all need attention? Have you ever thought about how the different parts of your life link up?

Inside *The Decasections of Life,* Wole explains that real success is only achieved when you are successful in all ten areas of your life. He breaks down each area of life and asks insightful questions throughout the book that will provoke you to reflect on your life, setting you on the path to true success. Once you start reading The Decasections of Life, you will see life differently and start to grasp everything that belongs to you. You cannot be the same again!

Another book from Decasections.org

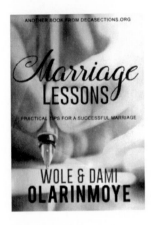

Marriage Lessons

Author: Wole & Dami Olarinmoye

ISBN-13: 978-1908588203

Format: Paperback, Pages: 104

Book information

'Marriage Lessons' is practical and outrightly down-to earth. In this thought-provoking and witty book, Wole and Dami Olarinmoye share valuable lessons from their personal experience of being 'single and seeking' and of the 'ups and sometimes not quite ups' of marriage. Single men and women will find useful tips for getting it right from the start and answers to some daunting situations. Finding the right partner is not enough; this book will help prepare you so that you yourself are Mr or Mrs Right.

Wole and Dami know how challenging marriage can be but yet show how exciting it can become once we learn to tango as a couple. They explore priceless themes which can tremendously enrich marriage like friendship and romance and, of course, sex. If you're bewildered by differences between you and your spouse, then you ought to read this book; it refocuses your mind on the beauty and complementary value of difference.

Another book from Decasections.org

Lessons From The Garden of Eden

Author: Wole Olarinmoye

ISBN-13: 9781908588326

Format: Paperback, Pages: 72

Book information

The Garden of Eden: the ultimate utopia, a place of peace and tranquility, paradise on earth. Have you ever thought about how idyllic life must have been in the Garden of Eden? Have you ever wondered what life would have been like if man did not fall into sin? Adam did not laze around Eden spending his days just plucking fruit from trees; he had an exciting, productive and fruitful life. In this book, Wole shows us that when Jesus redeemed us from the consequences of the fall, He restored us back to the Garden of Eden lifestyle. Several truths about the Garden of Eden lifestyle are directly applicable to us today as heirs of salvation. By applying these truths to our lives, we can enjoy the Garden of Eden life even today. It's a small book but it will change your perspective on life. Prepare to be blessed!

Another book from Decasections.org

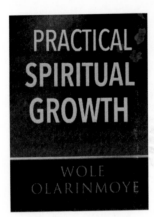

Practical Spiritual Growth

Author:Wole Olarinmoye Olarinmoye

ISBN-13: 978-1908588210

Format: Paperback, Pages: 136

Book information

'Practical Spiritual Growth gives fresh insight into the age-old topic of spiritual growth. It is practical, revealing and answers questions like: What does it really mean to grow spiritually? What does a spiritual person look like? What are the goals of spiritual growth? How do you kick-start growing spiritually? You will also find a whole section on how to choose the right church for you. In this book, Wole draws on his almost 25 years' experience as a Bible teacher and 21 years as a Christian professional, to focus on the three things that really matter in spiritual growth: your relationship with God, your relationship with His word and where you worship. Prepare to be blessed!

Notes

Notes

Notes

Notes